TIMELINES

1960s

by
Jane Duden

901214

CRESTWOOD HOUSE
New York

Library of Congress Cataloging In Publication Data
Duden, Jane.
    1960s / by Jane Duden.
    p. cm. — (Timelines)
    Includes index.
    Summary: History, trivia, and fun through photographs and articles present life
in the United States between 1960 and 1969.
    ISBN 0-89686-477-4
    1. United States—History—1961-1969—Juvenile literature. 2. History, Modern—
1945- —Juvenile literature. [1. United States—History—1961-1969—Miscellanea.] I.
Title. II. Title: Nineteen sixties. III. Series: Timelines (New York, N.Y.)
E841.D83   1989   973.923—dc20   89-34399
                                                                 CIP
                                                                 AC

Photo credits
Cover: The Bettmann Archive: The Beatles arrive in New York
FPG International: 4, 20 (left), 21, 22, 46; (J. Florea) 16
Wide World Photos: 7, 8, 11, 13, 14, 15, 18, 19, 20 (right), 23, 27, 28, 29, 31, 33, 34, 35, 37, 38,
    39, 40, 42, 43, 44
The Ford Motor Company: 24
The Bettmann Archive: 26, 30

Macmillan Publishing Company
866 Third Avenue
New York, NY 10022
Collier Macmillan Canada, Inc.

CRESTWOOD HOUSE

Produced by Carnival Enterprises

Printed in the United States of America

First Edition

10   9   8   7   6   5   4   3   2   1

CONTENTS

INTRODUCTION

The sixties were a time of challenge and change. They brought hippies, the Space Age, folk music, and the Beatles. Women's skirts got shorter, men's hair got longer, and almost everyone talked about love. But the sixties also brought turmoil.

Protests for civil rights and against the Vietnam War drew millions of people into the streets. Assassins took the lives of President John F. Kennedy, Dr. Martin Luther King, Jr., and Senator Robert F. Kennedy. In an era of new freedom, many young people tried drugs. It was the best of times and the worst of times. Life in America would never be quite the same again.

President John F. Kennedy (1917–1963)

BAREFOOT BIKILA

Abebe Bikila, Ethiopian marathon runner, lined up with the other 68 runners at the starting blocks. Bikila was not expected to even place in this 1960 Olympic long-distance race. His country had not produced many long-distance runners, and he was an unknown in the competition.

Used to training in the Ethiopian countryside, Bikila was sure to be affected by the cobblestoned route in Rome, especially since he would be barefoot. That was the way he was used to running.

Spectators along the route were shocked and amazed when they spotted Bikila's bare feet. Despite their doubts, they cheered him on. As it turned out, they were cheering for the winner— Abebe Bikila, gold medalist.

A GOLDEN MIRACLE

Winning three Olympic gold medals for Wilma Rudolph was more than an athletic victory — it was a miracle.

As a child, Wilma nearly died from scarlet fever and pneumonia. She survived, but doctors said she probably would never walk again. But Wilma and her family struggled and worked to make her legs stronger. After wearing braces and special shoes for many years, Wilma finally was on her own. What a joy it was to be able to run at last—faster and faster! Could she be the fastest? Her mother's words rang in her heart: "Never give up. Never give up." So Wilma Rudolph spent the next nine years trying. Then, on September 8, 1960, Wilma did it. She entered the Olympics in Rome.

Racing to her mother's "Never give up" and the crowd's wild cheers, Wilma crossed the finish line for her third gold medal of the Olympic Games.

Wilma Rudolph receives one of her gold medals at the 1960 Olympics.

John F. Kennedy (right) explains his views during the October 21 television debate with Richard Nixon.

THE GREAT DEBATE

For the first time in American history, TV played a big role in a presidential election. Senator John F. Kennedy was the "underdog." He was very young (43), not well known, and Catholic; the United States had never had a Catholic president. Richard M. Nixon had fame and experience as vice president under Eisenhower. But when the TV cameras rolled, the opinions of many Americans shifted. On the air, Nixon looked tired and haggard from months of campaigning. He often wiped sweat from his brow. To many viewers, he seemed nervous or evasive.

On the other side of the stage, Kennedy stood tall. He acted confident. His good looks and sense of humor changed many minds and votes. On November 8, Americans again relied on TV, this time for the election results. In the beginning, it looked like a tie. First Kennedy pulled ahead. Then Nixon moved into the lead. Results poured in all night, with the candidates neck and neck. The final vote was close: Kennedy with 34,221,344 votes and Nixon with 34,106,671. Americans had just elected their youngest president ever. Kennedy won by a nose.

SPACE PROGRAM SPIN-OFFS

Alarms from digital clocks wake us every morning. We fry eggs in Teflon pans. These things are spin-offs from the space program. So are modern football helmets, the fabric in the roofs of domed stadiums, hand-held calculators, and even the words "live via satellite." In 1960, the National Aeronautics and Space Administration (NASA) sent up ECHO, the first communications satellite that could be seen with the naked eye. Today we enjoy worldwide TV coverage, freeze-dried foods, plastic model train cars, and many toys and technological advancements for which we have the space program to thank!

OFF COURSE

In November, an American rocket launched from Cape Canaveral, Florida, strayed off course. It wound up in neighboring Cuba, where it crashed, killing a cow. The Cuban government used the event to embarrass the United States, its political foe. They gave the cow an official funeral. At the funeral, Cubans paid tribute to the cow as a victim of U.S. "imperialist aggression."

CAMELOT

Once upon a time, for a thousand days, Jack and Jacqueline Kennedy lived in the White House. The dashing young president moved into the mansion with his family. They brought two small children, dogs, a cat, three birds, three ponies, two hamsters, and a rabbit. The Kennedys' parties and balls added glamor to Washington.

In his inaugural speech to the nation, President Kennedy said "a new generation of Americans" would face the challenges of the sixties, which he called the New Frontier. He encouraged the young to act by saying, "Ask not what your country can do for you, but what you can do for your country." Soon, events at home and throughout the world would test all Americans.

Much later, Jacqueline Kennedy would describe those days. It was like Camelot, the magical castle of the legendary King Arthur. According to Mrs. Kennedy, her husband liked the popular song "Camelot" from the Broadway musical of the same name.

THE SPACE RACE IS ON!

The space race begun in 1957 by the launch of *Sputnik* was fueled again by another Soviet achievement. While the United States was still selecting, testing, and training its first astronauts, the Soviets sent the first man into space. On April 12, 1961, Yuri Gagarin made his famous orbit around Earth in one hour and forty-eight minutes.

Americans needed a space victory. It came on May 5, 1961. The spacecraft *Freedom 7* carried astronaut Alan Shepard into space. His fifteen-minute suborbital flight put the United States in the running for the space race. On May 25, President Kennedy urged the nation to commit itself to landing a man on the moon before the decade was out and returning him safely. The challenge was met in 1969.

10   *President and Mrs. John F. Kennedy bring their two children to the White House for the first time.*

BANANA BLADES

The hockey world was changed by accident during the 1960–1961 season. Stan Mikita of the Chicago Black Hawks noticed he was getting some strange shots from his stick. His shots and passes seemed to float, drop, and then curve. It gave him an advantage on the ice. Mikita checked his stick. He saw it was bent and cracked.

Others on the team liked what they saw from Mikita on the ice, bent stick and all. So they began to work on their own hockey sticks, hoping to imitate the banana-shaped curve of Mikita's stick. Players shoved their sticks under a door, leaving them bent overnight. With his new banana-blade stick, Bobby Hull, a teammate, could send a puck hurtling at 110 miles per hour! Together Bobby and Mikita got even more goals. They won the scoring championship six times.

But it didn't last. Goalies, the targets of these smashing shots, began to complain. The shots from these bent-up sticks were dangerous, they said. Hockey officials listened.

Today the curved hockey stick must meet official standards. A bent or curved banana-blade stick costs the offending player a penalty.

FIGHTING FIRE WITH FIRE

It was an inferno. The world's biggest gas fire began in November 1961. The blaze happened at Gassi Touil in the Sahara Desert. Flames from the fire shot as high as 450 feet. It seemed to burn forever, fueled by the limitless underground gas.

Paul "Red" Adair was called in to cap the gas line and stop the raging fire. He was a daring troubleshooter from Houston, Texas. Red studied the situation for weeks. What would he do?

Adair set off 550 pounds of dynamite to choke off the blaze. Fighting fire with fire worked. The dynamite blast used up the oxygen that fed the gas fire. The biggest gas fire in history was

12

Left: Joan Baez. Right: Bob Dylan

finally extinguished in April 1962. Putting it out earned Adair a cool $1 million.

Red Adair gained more fame when he was played by John Wayne in the Hollywood film *Hellfighters*. It showed the story of the raging fire in the Algerian desert.

TWIST AND SHOUT!

Chubby Checker, 19, had a hit when he sang, "Come on, baby, let's do the twist." American teens in the sixties were always inventing new dances. The dances had colorful names that were supposed to describe how they looked: the twist, jerk, pony, wiggle wobble, frug, and mashed potatoes were just a few. And everybody's *still* doing the loco-motion!

IN THE BABE'S FOOTSTEPS

New York Yankee Roger Maris finished the 1961 regular season with 61 homers, a single-season record. The 61st put him one ahead of Babe Ruth, whose record had stood for 34 years. The shy Maris had to be forced to take a bow before the fans.

STRUMMING STRINGS

More than 400,000 guitars were sold in the United States in 1961. The folk music boom of the early sixties made everyone want to strum guitars and become folksingers. Joan Baez and Bob Dylan wrote popular protest songs. They sang out against war and for civil rights.

1962

John Glenn poses for reporters before his historic flight aboard Friendship 7.

FIRST AMERICAN ORBITS EARTH:
THE SKY'S THE LIMIT!

Astronaut John Glenn became an instant American hero on February 20. In the tiny Mercury spacecraft named *Friendship 7*, Glenn made three orbits of the earth. He became America's first orbiting spaceman.

Glenn landed safely after a five-hour flight. Mission Control had some tense moments, though. There were concerns that *Friendship 7*'s heat shield might come loose. The heat shield protects the astronaut from the intense heat of reentry into Earth's atmosphere. Luckily, the heat shield stayed put.

When John Glenn came back to Earth, New Yorkers showered him with confetti. This "ticker tape" parade is named after the ribbons of telegraph paper New York financial district workers used to throw from their windows onto paraders below.

Wilt Chamberlain makes another basket.

14

WILT THE STILT'S SCORE SOARS

There was only one word for it: awesome! It was March 2, 1962. Philadelphia Warrior Wilton Norman Chamberlain ("Wilt the Stilt") toppled basketball records for the most points scored in one game. The Warriors and the New York Knicks were battling it out. The 7-foot, 3-inch basketball giant dropped 100 points through that hoop! The Warriors beat the Knicks 169 to 147.

WHOA! JOCKEY SAYS "ENOUGH!"

Jockey Eddie Arcaro retired April 3 as the greatest money-winning rider in horse-racing history. A jockey for 31 years, he crossed the finish line first in 4,779 races. Arcaro was also the first jockey to win racing's Triple Crown twice. You'd never guess that Eddie had a little trouble learning his trade. He lost 45 races in a row before guiding a horse to victory!

Marilyn Monroe

FALLEN STAR

One of Hollywood's most famous movie stars was found dead in her home at the age of 36. A bottle of sleeping pills lay by her side. It looked like suicide. Fans all over the world mourned her death. Years later, people are still fascinated by the life and death of an American original—Marilyn Monroe.

D-D-DANGER: DDT!

Scientist and writer Rachel Carson created a stir when she warned that if we weren't careful, our earth would slowly be killed by pollution. Plants and animals would die, and birds would no longer sing. Carson studied chemical pesticides that were developed to kill insects. The chemicals were building up in the earth's soil and water. They were building up in the bodies of animals. The chemicals destroyed not only harmful insects, but useful insects, too.

Rachel Carson grew more and more alarmed. Was no one thinking about the long-range effects of these chemicals? She wrote a book called *Silent Spring* in 1962 to warn people of the dangers of pesticides, especially DDT.

By the early seventies, at least five states had banned or limited the use of DDT. Rachel Carson's warning in *Silent Spring* saved generations of animals by alerting us to the dangers of pesticides.

THE CASE OF THE MISSING MINUS SIGN

On July 22, *Mariner I* was launched from Cape Canaveral, Florida. The spaceship was to provide the first close-up view of the planet Venus. But four minutes after takeoff, the spaceship crashed into the Atlantic.

Experts looked into the matter and found the cause—a minus sign had been omitted by mistake from the computer program. The computer gave the spaceship the wrong instructions. The single error cost the U.S. space program $18.5 million.

JACKIE ROBINSON ELECTED TO HALL OF FAME

Jackie Robinson was the first black American to play in major league baseball. His outstanding talent and determination won him a place in the Baseball Hall of Fame in 1962.

17

Martin Luther King, Jr.

EQUALITY IN SPACE

June 16, 1963, marked the beginning of sexual equality in space travel. Soviet cosmonaut Valentina Tereshkova became the first woman to travel into space. Her trip lasted three days. She made 49 orbits of Earth in the *Vostok 6*.

RONALD MCDONALD

Executives at the McDonald's hamburger chain were impressed by the man who played Bozo the Clown on Washington, D.C.'s WRC-TV. In 1963, they asked him to create a new clown for McDonald's commercials. The result was the fun-loving "Ronald McDonald." He appeared all over Washington for many years. Then McDonald's decided to have the clown perform nationally—but not with the original actor. McDonald's advertising agency said the person who created Ronald was wrong for the part.

At first, the actor was disappointed. But eventually he made it to national television on his own. His name is Willard Scott, the well-known "Today Show" weatherman.

18 *Martin Luther King, Jr., addresses the huge crowd that gathered in front of the Lincoln Memorial in August 1963.*

"I HAVE A DREAM"

On August 28, 1963, more than 200,000 peaceful demonstrators filled Washington, D.C. They came to demand the passage of civil rights laws, or equal rights for blacks and whites. It was the largest protest of its kind in the capital's history. On this date, the civil rights leader Dr. Martin Luther King, Jr., gave what has become one of the most famous speeches in American history:

> I have a dream that my four little children will one day live in a nation where they will not be judged by the color of their skin but by the content of their character. . . .

King dreamed that racial prejudice would be defeated, and that one day his people would be able to say, "free at last, free at last, thank God Almighty, we are free at last."

Left: President and Mrs. John F. Kennedy arrive in Dallas, Texas.
Right: After the president was shot, Mrs. Kennedy leans over her husband's
body while their car races to the hospital.

A NATION MOURNS

President Kennedy was struck and killed by an assassin's bullet as he rode in a parade in Dallas, Texas, on November 22. The news flashed across the continent. Millions of Americans hunched in disbelief over radios and TVs. Bells tolled. Silent crowds gathered in churches.

Just 99 minutes after the president died, Vice President Lyndon B. Johnson was sworn in as our 36th president. The oath was given aboard the presidential plane at an airport in Dallas.

The plane flew back to Washington, D.C., with the dead president, Mrs. Kennedy, and the new president aboard.

The country's feeling of loss was summed up by a riderless horse named Black Jack that marched in President Kennedy's funeral. Black Jack walked behind the casket, wearing an empty saddle. A pair of rider's boots were reversed in the stirrups. This showed a leader had fallen and would never ride again.

Kennedy's accused assassin, Lee Harvey Oswald, was never brought to trial. Police were moving Oswald to a different jail when he was shot by a man named Jack Ruby. As a result, no one knows for sure who killed President Kennedy.

John F. Kennedy died thirty minutes after he was shot. His funeral took place in Washington, D.C., on November 25.

1964

BEATLEMANIA!

Thousands of shrieking fans waited at New York's Kennedy Airport in February for the arrival of the British rock and roll band the Beatles. The long-haired "Fab Four" were played on radio stations all over the world. "I want to hold your hand" and "Yeah, yeah, yeah," words from their songs, became famous. Later that month, the Beatles appeared on the "Ed Sullivan Show." They performed sold-out concerts in Carnegie Hall. The frenzy over the rock group, known as Beatlemania, was just beginning.

POP ART

Imagine becoming rich and famous for painting giant Brillo boxes and Campbell's soup cans. That's what Andy Warhol did. Warhol was called the pioneer of pop art.

Pop art showed people a new way of looking at things in the world around them. Popsters said advertising, movies, TV, cars,

The Beatles meet Ed Sullivan.

Andy Warhol, with model Robin MacDonald (left) and artist Jane Wagner, poses with his latest work, titled Brillo.

even supermarkets, should be considered art. Others disagreed and said pop art was not inspiring.

Everybody noticed the wild exhibition Warhol held in a New York art gallery in 1964. The gallery was made to look like a supermarket. People had trouble telling Warhol's art from the real products! As it turned out, one big difference was the price. Andy Warhol's famous Campbell's soup cans sold for $1,500 a piece.

POETRY IN MOTION

When Cassius Clay entered the world of boxing, he became one of the most controversial athletes of the century. No one denied that he packed a walloping punch with his 220-pound frame. On February 25, 1964, he defeated Sonny Liston to become the heavyweight champion of the world. But some people didn't like his bragging. He had a habit of saying such things as,

"I am the greatest of all time. I am the prettiest." He also insulted his opponents in rhyme.

Cassius Clay surprised some people even more when he became a Black Muslim and took the name Muhammad Ali.

Then in 1967 Ali refused to serve in the military for religious reasons, and arguments about the heavyweight grew heated. He was stripped of his title by the World Boxing Association. The Supreme Court later ruled he was entitled to refuse the draft on religious grounds. Ali went into the ring again and eventually regained his title. Many boxing fans believe that Muhammad Ali is still "the greatest."

UP IN SMOKE

The first time the U.S. government warned people that cigarette smoke could be harmful was in 1964. That was the first year the line "Cigarette smoking may be hazardous to your health" was put on cigarette packs.

The government warning angered the powerful tobacco industry. Tobacco farmers and cigarette manufacturers alike depended on people's smoking habits to make money. The news that cigarette smoking was linked to cancer was bad news for them.

Since then, scientific research has shown that smoking can cause heart attacks and birth defects, as well as cancer. Many cigarette companies still argue, however, that smoking is safe.

MUSTANGS CHARGE OUT OF MICHIGAN

Ford's Mustang rolled into auto showrooms in late April. With a price tag of $2,368, it was sporty and affordable. Lee A. Iacocca was the genius behind the Mustang. The car set an all-time record for first-year sales of a new model.

SIGNED INTO LAW

On July 2 the most sweeping civil rights legislation in the history of the United States became law. It was called the Civil Rights Act of 1964. Racial discrimination was prohibited on the job, in public places, in government-owned facilities, unions, and federally funded programs. President Johnson said the days of denying equal rights to America's 22 million blacks were over.

A SCORE FOR THE OTHER TEAM

Jim Marshall of the Minnesota Vikings holds the record for playing the most pro football games in a row—282. But that's not his only claim to fame. On October 28, 1964, the San Francisco 49ers and the Vikings were playing a tense game. Jim saw the other team fumble and rushed to scoop up the loose ball. Forgetting where his team's goal was, Jim ran 60 yards the wrong way and scored a safety and two points for the other side. Not until a player on the 49ers came to say thanks did he realize his blunder. But the Vikings won anyway, 27–22.

A LOPSIDED ELECTION

President Johnson was elected in 1964. He defeated Senator Barry Goldwater in one of the biggest landslide elections in American history. President Johnson brought one of his pet beagles, Him, to the inaugural parade the following January. No other White House pet had been so honored.

The 1964 Ford Mustang

1965

WHAT'S FOR LUNCH?

What's your favorite brown-bag lunch? A peanut butter sandwich? Ham and cheese on rye? Astronaut John Young decided he wanted to bring his favorite lunch on the flight he took with fellow astronaut Virgil "Gus" Grissom on March 31, 1965.

At the end of their orbital flight, one of the dehydrated astronaut meals was found uneaten. Had one of the astronauts skipped a meal? No, Young had smuggled a bologna sandwich on board and eaten it instead!

THE SOUND OF MUSIC

By 1965, some people were ready for something to take their minds off riots, war, protests, and civil rights struggles. Along came *The Sound of Music.* It was a film about romantic love, parental love, duty, and patriotism. The movie musical starred sunny Julie Andrews. In 1965 and 1966, it was shown in 3,200 theaters around the world. One woman in Wales went to see it every day for a year.

Julie Andrews and cast members of The Sound of Music.

TAKING BASEBALL INDOORS

When the Houston Astrodome opened on April 9, sports fans called it the eighth wonder of the world. It was the world's first roofed stadium. No more rain outs! The only problem was the eighth wonder had over 4,596 faults. That was the number of see-through plastic panels in the dome.

The problem showed up during the first baseball game played in the dome. The sun shining through the panels created a glare. Players looking up to catch fly balls were temporarily blinded. Not only that, but the pattern of girders further hid balls in the air. What to do? The glaring mistake in the dome's design was solved by painting the panels a dark color. The paint shut out the sun, and the teams could see the fly balls again.

GOOD GRIEF!

Snoopy had a crush on Twiggy. Why not? Both were bright stars in the 1960s pop culture. In the mid-sixties, the "Peanuts" cartoon gang zoomed in popularity. Then in 1965, "Peanuts" came to TV. "A Charlie Brown Christmas" was the first of many TV specials to air. The star was and is Snoopy's master, Charlie Brown, who was always messing up. The gang also included the bad-tempered Lucy, the musician Schroeder, and Linus, famous for clinging to his blanket. But there never has been a character named Peanuts in the comic strip!

Below left: Astronaut John Young. Right: Twiggy

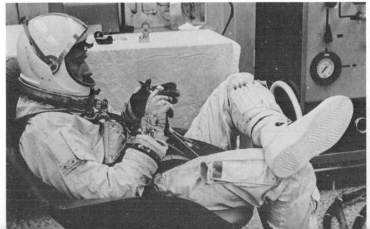

1965

1965

TWO RECORDS IN ONE DAY

It was the eighth perfect game in baseball history. A game in which no rival players reached first base, it happened on September 9. Los Angeles Dodger Sandy Koufax pitched a perfect game for a 1–0 victory over the Chicago Cubs. That's not all! It was a no-hitter, also. Sandy Koufax became the first in baseball history ever to pitch four no-hitters. It was his fourth no-hit game in four years.

WAR CRIES

The war in Vietnam was troubling Americans more and more. Television brought the war into our own living rooms on the news each evening. By the end of 1965, 190,000 American servicemen and women had gone to Vietnam. Of these, 1,350 had died and 5,300 had been injured.

Protests took place daily. College students led antiwar marches and sit-ins. Many young men burned their draft cards. Families and communities disagreed about whether U.S. troops should be fighting in Southeast Asia. Many felt it was not patriotic to go against the war. Others felt it was necessary to speak out against the killing. On October 15, 1965, more than 10,000 protesters marched down Fifth Avenue in New York City. But the war went on.

L.A. Dodger Sandy Koufax holds up four balls to indicate his four no-hit games.

WHO TURNED OUT THE LIGHTS?

Traffic signals gave out and intersections jammed. Skyscraper elevators stopped between floors, trapping people for hours. Airplanes circled darkened landing strips. What had happened?

Nine northeastern states and parts of Canada were plunged into sudden darkness during the worst power failure in history. Everything electrical sputtered to a standstill. Lights dimmed and went out. Thousands of Easterners were left in the dark, some for as long as 13 hours.

For them, November 9 was the night the world stood still. It was known as the "blackout."

Computers lost their memories. Airports shut down. Food spoiled in refrigerators. Mail stacked up in dark post offices. At one hospital, a doctor broke out of a dark operating room. He groped down seven flights of stairs to get flashlights so surgeons could finish a critical operation.

War protesters picketed in many places, even in front of the White House in Washington, D.C.

1966

TV'S NEW SUPERHERO

On January 12, one out of every three homes tuned in to "Batman," the new hit on TV. It was the highest rating since the Beatles appeared on the "Ed Sullivan Show" in February 1964.

TV's dynamic duo of Batman (Adam West) and Robin (Burt Ward) were incredibly popular. People were batty about the characters who lived by the Boy Scout Code. They loved reading the comical *splats* and *biffs* during fights between Batman and his enemies: AARGH! CLASH! KLONK! POW! CLUNK! EEE-YOW! KAPOW! This once-popular show is still in reruns. And a new movie version came to theaters in 1989.

BEAM ME UP!

"Star Trek" was at the bottom of the ratings during its first season, 1966. Few guessed it would become the most popular science fiction show in the history of television.

Television's Batman and Robin

Left: William Shatner (left), DeForest Kelley (center), and Leonard Nimoy, three of the stars of "Star Trek." Right: Astronaut Neil Armstrong

In fact, in 1969 "Star Trek" was canceled. Because most of its loyal viewers were teenagers, advertisers weren't willing to spend money on the show. But the "Star Trek" story was just beginning.

The show became even more popular after it was canceled, and eventually went into reruns. A series of Star Trek movies followed. Star Trek fans, who call themselves "trekkies," now enjoy a new TV series: "Star Trek: The Next Generation."

A CLOSE CALL

Somewhere over Red China and seven hours into the mission, *Gemini 8* started to tumble and toss violently. Astronauts Neil Armstrong and Major David Scott could not get the spacecraft under control. They were ordered to ditch the mission and splash down in the Pacific. They were 60 hours ahead of plan, but the astronauts landed safely and lived to try it again.

THE RUNNER'S DISGUISE

On the third Monday in April, Roberta Bingay put her secret plan into action. Wearing a hooded sweatshirt to disguise the fact that she was female, she hid in the bushes near the starting line.

When the starting gun sounded, Roberta jumped out and joined the other runners—all men—in the famous Boston Marathon.

At the time, only men were allowed to enter the race. But Roberta was determined. She had ridden a bus to Boston from her home in California and was ready for this race. As she ran, the sweatshirt became too warm. She took off her disguise, and the crowd discovered a woman running with the 415 men!

Roberta ran the race in 3 hours, 21 minutes. She was the 124th person to cross the finish line. Roberta had proven that women were strong enough to run all 26 miles of the marathon. Better still, six years later the rules of the marathon were changed to include women. Since then, thousands of women have followed Roberta's lead and run the distance.

A NEW ACT FOR REAGAN

A heavy voter turnout helped Ronald Reagan begin a new career on November 8. The 55-year-old former movie actor won his first try for public office when he was elected governor of California.

FAREWELL, WALT DISNEY

Almost everyone has a favorite Disney film, Disney song, or Disney character. Some people have several! Entertainment genius Walt Disney died of cancer on December 15. But his influence and dreams will live on.

Between 1920 and 1950, Walt Disney created animated film techniques and effects others had barely dreamed of. He also

32 *Left: Walt Disney. Right: Cowboy movie star Roy Rogers riding his famous horse, Trigger*

gave us some of the world's best-loved characters—Mickey Mouse, Donald Duck, Goofy, and Pluto. Then there was his success in filmmaking. Since its release in 1937, *Snow White and the Seven Dwarfs* has become one of the most popular movies in history. The Disney studio has won more than 45 Academy Awards for its movies and for scientific and technical ideas in filmmaking.

TRIGGER, WONDER HORSE FOREVER

Roy Rogers's horse, Trigger, will be around for your grandchildren to see. When Trigger died at age 33, Rogers had him stuffed and mounted for display. Trigger was a golden palomino who had appeared in 87 movies and more than 100 episodes of the 1950s television show starring Roy Rogers.

Roy really loved Trigger. When Trigger died, Roy said, "It was like losing one of the family. During all those hard rides for pictures and television, he never fell once. We had to do more retakes for human actors than for Trigger."

GLYPHS

Expo '67, a huge fair held in Montreal, Canada, drew visitors from all over the world. It also faced a problem: How could they accommodate people who speak and read so many different languages?

Then someone came up with the idea of using glyphs. They were signs and symbols that everyone could understand immediately. Eventually, Expo '67 developed twenty-four signs without words for its international visitors. Symbols for DON'T LITTER, BUS STATION, DON'T TOUCH, and COFFEE SHOP were a few. Many of these signs and symbols have now been accepted around the world.

SAD DAY FOR AMERICAN SPACE PROGRAM

On January 27, astronauts Virgil Grissom, Edward White, and Roger Chaffee were killed in a flash fire as they sat in their *Apollo 1* spacecraft. They were performing a routine ground test. Experts investigated why the fire happened. They found 113 major errors in the building of the capsule. The capsule was redesigned, and the space race took off again.

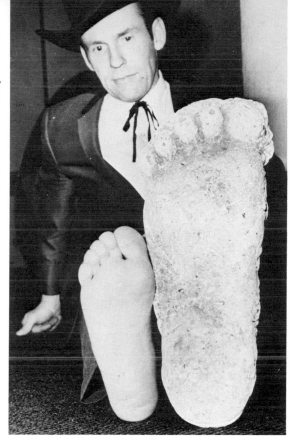

Roger Patterson compares his foot with a plaster cast that he said was taken from Bigfoot's footprint.

MYSTERIOUS MONSTER

"My! What big feet you have!" That's what Roger Patterson and Bob Gimlin might have said when they took one of the only films of the legendary Bigfoot on October 20.

Native Americans called the monster Sasquatch. Patterson and Gimlin were in the woods near Bluff Creek, California. Suddenly their horses snorted, rolled their eyes, and reared. The men spotted a movement in the distance, grabbed the movie camera, aimed, and filmed. Was it Bigfoot? Or had a local prankster dressed up to give tourists a thrill? The men don't think so. A pungent odor, giant footprints, and the movie film told them they'd finally seen Bigfoot.

During a practice session in the Apollo 1 *spacecraft, astronauts Roger Chaffee (left), Edward White (center), and Virgil Grissom were killed in a flash fire.*

35

SUPER BOWL SUCCESS

The Super Bowl was born in 1967. The Green Bay Packers beat the Kansas City Chiefs, 35–10. The best team from the National Football Conference was pitted against the best team from the American Football Conference. The Super Bowl has become so popular that advertisers pay hundreds of thousands of dollars for commercials when it is broadcast.

FIRST HEART TRANSPLANT

Louis Washkansky, the world's first heart-transplant patient, died December 21 in Cape Town, South Africa. He had managed, though, to live for 18 days with the heart of a 25-year-old woman beating in his chest. The surgery was performed by Dr. Christiaan Barnard. The new heart, from a woman who had been killed in a car accident, beat strongly, but the 53-year-old grocer died of lung problems. It was the beginning of a new medical miracle—organ transplant.

HEAVY, HAIRY, AND GROOVY

In the sixties, kids had a language of their own. For example, to "freak out" meant to lose touch with reality or lose control. A "freak" was someone very involved with a certain thing, like a music freak or a food freak. "Groovy" meant terrific, great. "Hairy" was frightening. To get "hung up" was to be unable to make a decision, or it could mean getting absorbed in an activity, as in "I got hung up with homework and missed the TV show." "Heavy" meant profound or meaningful. "Flower power" was the idea of changing the world through peace and love. A "flower child" was a "hippie," or someone who tried to live in a natural and simple way. "Different strokes for different folks" meant each person was entitled to his or her own likes, dislikes, and opinions.

Flower children and hippies at a love-in in Cincinnati

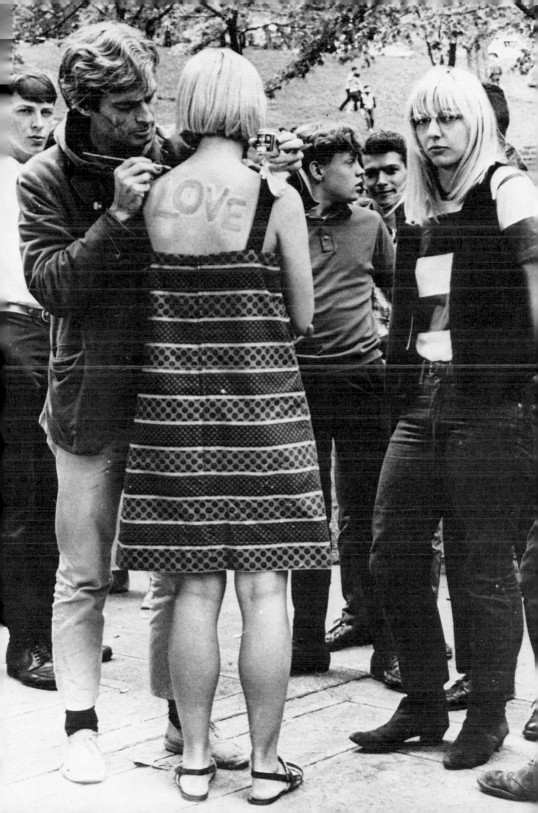

1968

DEMOCRATIC CONVENTION BREAKS INTO RIOTS

In a hot August in Chicago, the convention to nominate the Democratic candidate for president of the United States turned into a four-day-long police riot. Demonstrators gathered by the thousands outside the convention center where Vice President Hubert Humphrey had just been chosen to run for president. The demonstrators were there to protest against the Vietnam War.

Police attacked the crowds with clubs and tear gas. More than 100 people were hurt, and many more were arrested. Millions saw the fighting and violence on their televisions. It was a summer of anger as feelings about the Vietnam War grew hotter and hotter.

Peace demonstrators hold up their hands in the peace sign before the Illinois National Guardsmen outside the Conrad Hilton, the Democratic Convention headquarters, in Chicago.

President-elect Richard Nixon (center) celebrates after the 1968 election.

PRESIDENTIAL FIRSTS

Richard M. Nixon lost his first try for the United States presidency when John F. Kennedy won the 1960 election. He tried again in 1968 and won.

Nixon became a president who achieved some unique firsts. He was the first United States president to visit the U.S.S.R. and the first U.S. president to visit China. Later, in his second term of office, he became the first U.S. president to resign.

A CLASSY CAR

On October 14, 1968, the Secret Service received a special delivery. It was a new car—a 1969 Presidential Lincoln Continental Executive. The "options" drove the price up a bit. The car was almost 22 feet long. An extra two tons of armor plate were added. And the inner rubber-edged steel disc tires were a must. They guaranteed that even if all four tires were shot out, the car could still travel at 50 miles per hour. What was the final price of this classy car? $500,000!

HE PROMISED HER THE MOON

According to Greek tradition, rain on a wedding day is good luck. It certainly looked like a lucky day for Jacqueline Kennedy. On a rainy October 20 she married one of the world's richest men, Aristotle Onassis of Greece. During their first year of marriage, he gave her jewelry worth more than $5 million. Their glamorous marriage made headlines throughout the world.

ANOTHER FIRST FOR BLACKS

Shirley Chisholm was a Brooklyn nursery school teacher who switched careers. That in itself is not unusual. But Chisholm went on to earn the distinction of becoming America's first black woman elected to Congress. November 5, 1968, was a day for black Americans and all women to celebrate.

Aristotle Onassis and Jacqueline Kennedy after their wedding in Greece

HE DIDN'T WANT TO EAT JUST ONE

Paul G. Tully of Brisbane University in Australia had no intention of eating just one potato chip! He chomped through 30 two-ounce bags in 24 minutes and 33.6 seconds to set a world record in May 1969. Paul munched that bunch without drinking any liquid!

HAPPILY EVER AFTER . . . EVENTUALLY

Adults often tell young people, "Wait to get married. Take your time." Octavio Guillen and Adriana Martinez must have heard that advice and decided to follow it. Their engagement lasted 67 years! When they finally decided to marry in June 1969, in Mexico City, they were each 82 years old!

TUNES

This year's movies gave us songs that are still heard often. "Raindrops Keep Falling on My Head" came from the movie *Butch Cassidy and the Sundance Kid*. Steppenwolf's "Born to Be Wild" accompanied Dennis Hopper and Peter Fonda riding a motorcycle in the movie *Easy Rider.* "Hello Dolly" came from Barbra Streisand's movie of the same name. The Beatles' "Come Together" was big in 1969. And Peter, Paul and Mary sang about "Leaving on a Jet Plane" in the year that gave us the Boeing 747 jumbo jet.

Switch-hitter Mickey Mantle

A SWITCH-HITTING STAR RETIRES

Mickey Mantle began hitting a baseball at the tender age of two. His father was right when he predicted his son would be as well known as the president of the United States. Mantle became a "switch-hitter," practicing with both left and right hands, when he was very young. He did that so he could hit well against both right- and left-handed pitchers.

Mickey loved all sports and was a star athlete in high school. Unfortunately, he was kicked in the leg during a football game. The injury caused Mickey to suffer from a serious bone disease for the rest of his career. That wasn't the only worry on Mantle's mind. He also feared dying from Hodgkin's disease, the illness that took the lives of both his father and grandfather when they were only 39. So, Mickey Mantle played each game with energy, always wondering how long he would be able to play.

Switch-hitter Mantle belted 536 homers for the New York Yankees. He led the league in home runs four times. He was named Most Valuable Player in 1956, 1957, and 1962. Fans were sad to see him retire in 1969. Baseball card collectors today are willing to pay between $5,000 and $6,000 for one of his 1951 or 1952 rookie cards.

Peter, Paul and Mary

WOODSTOCK: YOUTH HAPPENING OF THE DECADE

In the summer of 1969, nearly a half million people made their way to a 600-acre farm in New York. They braved traffic jams, food and water shortages, and rainy weather. Why? To listen to rock music, wallow happily in mud, and do what they couldn't do at home. Many of the sixties' top rock musicians were there: Richie Havens, Jefferson Airplane, the Grateful Dead, Crosby, Stills, Nash and Young, the Who, and Jimi Hendrix. Much to the surprise of adults, the Woodstock Music and Arts Fair was a peaceful event. The three-day, nonstop outdoor rock concert was a weekend of music, love, and peace.

TAKE A NUMBER FOR WAR

The draft lottery was begun in 1969. Men were called up to military service if their number came up with local draft boards. The lottery was one way to get soldiers for the war in Vietnam. Protests continued against the most unpopular war in our history.

TO THE MOON!

One of the most sensational events in history took place on July 20, 1969. After a four-day journey in space, *Apollo 11* astronauts landed on the moon at 4:18 P.M., eastern daylight time. Six hours later Neil Armstrong took the first historic steps on the moon's surface, saying, "That's one small step for a man, one giant leap for mankind."

By one estimate, 600 million people watched the moonwalk on television. That was about one-fifth of the Earth's population. Even in nations unfriendly to America, the moon landing was cheered. A radio station in Cairo, Egypt, called it "the greatest human achievement ever." And a famous actress said nothing in show business would ever top what she saw on television that day. Chances are someone you know saw it and can tell you what they thought!

The American flag has flown on the moon since that July day. A plaque was also left on the moon, attached to the landing craft's descent stage. It reads:

HERE MEN FROM THE PLANET EARTH

FIRST SET FOOT UPON THE MOON

JULY 1969, A.D.

WE CAME IN PEACE FOR ALL MANKIND

The rock and soil samples from *Apollo 11* and other expeditions showed the moon to be more than four billion years old. These also proved the moon is and always was without life. Neil Armstrong's footprints remain as evidence of humankind's venture onto another world.

After Apollo 11 *lands on the moon, Edwin Aldrin walks on the surface.*   45

INDEX

Demonstrators protest the Vietnam War